Killerton

Successive e[obscured] the family, ar[obscured] the 1st Barone[obscured] 1655. 'Hugh t[obscured] advantageously, became the MP for [obscured] and sat for a portrait by Lely. In 1680 he made Killerton the principal family mansion, in preference to Columb John.

The menfolk of the Acland family pursued careers in politics from the Elizabethan era to the middle of the 20th century, often supporting liberal causes. They also became landowners of great influence throughout Devon, Cornwall and Somerset.

headquarters when Exeter was being besieged. Lady Acland wrote to Cromwell thanking him for taking great care of their home. Despite this the Aclands were fined £1,727 for having supported the king, a fine that was considered too lenient by one Parliamentarian, Richard Evans.

Above John Acland was the owner of Columb John and son of the 1st Baronet. His stone effigy is in Broadclyst Church

Right Sir Hugh Acland, 5th Baronet, by Peter Lely, c.1672

'Aclandshire'

By the 18th century, the legend arose that it was possible to walk from the English Channel to the Bristol Channel without leaving Acland property. 'Aclandshire', as it became known, was largely created by judicious marriages into other wealthy families.

Money and marriage

Two significant marriages brought great wealth to the Aclands. Hugh, the 6th Baronet (1697–1728) married Cecily Wroth in 1721, acquiring 2,300 acres near Bridgwater, and a dowry of £12,000 and his son, Sir Thomas, the 7th Baronet (1722–85) married Elizabeth Dyke of Tetton near Taunton. In return, she brought three Somerset estates (Holnicote,

Left *The Pastor's Fireside* by Henry Singleton depicts Sir Thomas Dyke Acland, 10th Baronet (far right) and his family being read to by the vicar of Silverton

Below left Thomas Dyke Acland, 9th Baronet, as a boy by Richard Phelps, c.1760

Below right Major Acland by Joshua Reynolds, 1769–71

Right *Lady Harriet Fox-Strangways, Mrs Acland, Crossing the River Hudson to the American Lines, Presenting Her Safe Conduct* by Robert Pollard, *c.*1777

Pixton and Tetton) to the family's holdings. She also added the name 'Dyke' to the family, so they became 'Dyke Acland'. Thomas was a typical 'sporting squire', with a passion for stag-hunting, drinking, gambling, cock-fighting and amorous adventures.

Death and disaster

Sir Thomas resolved to tackle the estate at Killerton, engaging John Veitch to lay out a park and commissioning a 'temporary' house from the architect John Johnson while awaiting the creation of a Palladian mansion to the designs of James Wyatt. The foundations were laid, but Thomas's plans were undermined by fate.

His son and heir, John Dyke Acland, had married Lady Harriet Fox-Strangways, daughter of the first Earl of Ilchester. As the American Revolution loomed, John became a Major in the British army and was sent to Canada; Harriet insisted on sailing with him. John Acland was wounded and taken prisoner at the second battle of Saratoga, and Harriet braved considerable dangers to nurse him back to health, behind enemy lines. They returned to Britain as celebrities, and Major Acland was received by George III. However, John's health had been compromised by his battlefield injuries, and he died in mysterious circumstances in 1778 at the age of 34, possibly as a result of a duel. He left Harriet bereft till her own death in 1815, some 37 years later.

The death of his eldest son and a disastrous fire at Holnicote were savage blows for Sir Thomas, and he abandoned his former plans for a grand new house. On his death in 1785 the estates passed to his grandson, who died at the tender age of seven, just weeks after inheriting. The estates then passed on to Thomas's estranged son, the 9th Baronet, also called Thomas. He was renowned for his gambling debts and passion for stag-hunting. His marriage to Henrietta Hoare, of the wealthy banking family, provided much-needed funds.

'Great Sir Thomas'

Their eldest son, the 10th Baronet, inherited both Killerton and his mother's intelligence in 1794 and deserved the epithet 'Great Sir Thomas'. His land holdings were increased when the Arundell family, lacking a male heir, traced the family tree back to an Acland daughter who had married into the family at the time of the Civil War. Trerice in Cornwall and the Arundell estate on Exmoor were added to Sir Thomas's estates.

Building Killerton

There has been a house on this site since 1610, and a map of 1756 reveals an H-shaped building with a formal garden and an orchard surrounded by fields. Hedgerows divided the land around the house into small or large fields. Each field was given its own name, making it very similar to a traditional farmhouse.

Two architects

Sir Thomas Dyke Acland, the 7th Baronet, commissioned the celebrated architect James Wyatt to design a new house for him in 1775. However, the relationship was not harmonious and, despite Wyatt's drawings for a grand Palladian-style mansion and foundations being laid, after three years Sir Thomas engaged a new architect, John Johnson.

Johnson also worked in the neoclassical idiom and was recommended as being 'exceedingly cheap and ingenious'. His house was intended as a 'stopgap'; Sir Thomas had wanted Wyatt's design erected at the top of the hill, while he and the family lived in the more modest house on the lower slopes. Work got underway in summer 1778 and was completed in June 1779.

Johnson designed a simple, well-proportioned rectangular two-storey house, with a flat roof and parapet. It had a pedimented entrance on the south side, giving onto a central corridor, off which were the four principal ground-floor rooms.

Extending the house

As a result of the death of Sir Thomas's eldest son and the fire at Holnicote in 1779, there were numerous money difficulties and Wyatt's grandiose house was never built. Instead, the Aclands' 'temporary residence' became permanent, and was greatly modified. Extra rooms were added as the family grew in size and prosperity. A large projecting window bay was added by the 10th Baronet in 1820. He also added bedrooms and a nursery to the first floor at the back of the house; these were level with the rising ground, so that the children and their nannies could enter the gardens and grounds easily, without tramping through the house. (These rooms are now used as offices by the National Trust.)

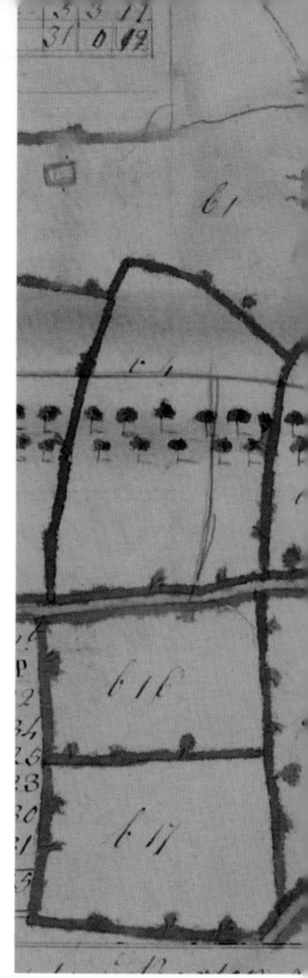

Far left John Johnson, the architect of Killerton

Below Unexecuted design for the south elevation of Killerton by James Wyatt

Above This 1756 map of Killerton shows the house in the centre with orchards and fields surrounding it

In the late 1890s, the house was modernised by Mr Protheroe, an architect from Cheltenham, for Sir Charles Dyke Acland to make it fit for country house parties with an improved layout, electricity, heating and bathrooms. The projecting single-storey wing on the north side of the house was intended as a combined office, study and billiard room and completed in 1900. The house was completely rejuvenated and cost over £8,000. Charles and his wife Gertrude now felt they had a house worthy of their position. The final major addition was the entrance porch, built in 1924 by Sir Francis Dyke Acland, the 14th Baronet, following a major fire in the house. The architect was Randall Wells and the low ceiling and arched doorway are typical of his Arts and Crafts style.

Right The Entrance Hall

The 19th century

'Great Sir Thomas'

'Great Sir Thomas' (1787–1871) earned his soubriquet through his public work and role as a benevolent patriarch. A committed Christian, as an MP he supported the Reform Bill and Catholic Emancipation. He also campaigned against the 'horrible and infamous' slave trade.

He founded schools at Killerton, Broadclyst and Selworthy and supported former servicemen left destitute after the Napoleonic wars. He was concerned by the agricultural depression which afflicted rural Britain and sought to encourage informal debate between politicians by co-founding the Grillion's Club, a dining club for MPs of all parties.

Sir Thomas married his third cousin, Lydia Hoare, of the famous banking family, in 1808. They had an income of £10,000 a year and extensive estates. The Aclands chose to live mostly at Killerton, instigating a major programme of works under the control of the versatile John Veitch. A new bow-fronted dining room was created, seating 20 people. Highly musical, Lydia had an organ built by popular organ-maker William Gray, along with a very recent innovation, a *pianoforte*.

Lady Lydia and Sir Thomas had ten children, three girls and seven boys, and took their role as parents very seriously. They were a high-achieving family. One son, Henry, became a baronet for his work in medicine and another, John Barton, emigrated to New Zealand where he established huge sheep stations and a new Acland dynasty.

The Aclands were enthusiastic travellers. On their two-masted schooner *The Lady of St Kilda* they circumnavigated the British mainland and travelled around the Mediterranean.

In memoriam

Sir Thomas was highly regarded locally. After his death, a monument was erected on the estate by his many admirers, and a popular song, *The Killerton Oak*, written by the local postmaster, included the lines:

His council was wise and firm as an oak
He did what was right and 'twas true what he spoke

Left Lydia, Lady Acland, depicted in a portrait miniature attributed to George Sanders (or Saunders), *c.*1808

'Tom Thumb'

Following the death of 'Great Sir Thomas' in 1871, his eldest son inherited at the age of 62. Known as 'Tom Thumb' – because he was junior to his father, Thomas the 10th Baronet – the 11th Baronet (1809–98) had become an MP in 1837 and supported the call for a national education system. Passionate about promoting education and good practice in agriculture, Sir Thomas helped revive the Bath and West Show. He bore the loss of his wife and daughter stoically when they died of scarlet fever in 1851. Both his sons were also politicians; Charles was MP for Launceston, Cornwall, and Arthur MP for Rotherham in Yorkshire. Sir Thomas died in 1898 and his elder son Charles became the 12th Baronet, inheriting 16,000 acres in Somerset, 15,000 in Devon and 5,000 in Cornwall.

Left Portrait bust of Sir Thomas Dyke Acland, 10th Baronet, by Edward Bowring Stephens

Above Sir Thomas Dyke Acland, 11th Baronet, by Cyrus Johnson, *c.*1883

The early 20th century

Sir Charles Dyke Acland

When Charles Dyke Acland took over at Killerton in 1898, the family fortunes had been depleted by marriage settlements, electioneering and the agricultural depression. Nevertheless, he was still the second largest landowner in Somerset, one of the top ten in Devon, and owned extensive holdings in Cornwall.

Killerton was the centre of this business empire, but Sir Charles and his wife Lady Gertrude found it hopelessly old-fashioned. Heating was limited to open fires, with candles and oil lamps the only lighting. Sanitary arrangements were rudimentary. Country house weekends were becoming popular, so the Aclands created a luxurious place to entertain their political friends, at a cost of £8,000. A new porch was added to the side of the house, and a broad gravel carriage drive. The former entrance-lobby and morning room were combined, creating a grand drawing room. The dining room became a large hall with a mighty oak staircase. The plain ceilings were decorated in neoclassical style, and low-relief plaster portraits of Sir Charles and Lady Gertrude were added to the ceiling in the dining room.

The first gift

The estate was still run on traditional lines, but in one respect Charles was very far-sighted. In 1917 he gave a 500-year lease for '7 or 8 thousand acres' of Exmoor to the National Trust. The gift guaranteed to the Aclands 'all the rents and profits and all the rights and powers of an owner but not the right to develop the land', in order to conserve it for future generations. This visionary gesture predated that of Charles's great-nephew, Sir Richard Dyke Acland, by nearly 30 years.

Left Late 19th-century photograph of Charles and Gertrude

Opposite Sir Francis Dyke Acland, 14th Baronet, by John Archibald Alexander Berrie, 1920

Photographs top to bottom

Eleanor and Francis celebrate the Liberal Party's victory at Tiverton in 1923

Summer house party at Killerton in 1929. Eleanor is far left in the middle row and Francis is third from left on the bottom row

Lloyd George making his speech at Killerton in 1925

A Liberal couple

Sir Charles and Lady Gertrude were childless, so on his death in 1919, the estate passed to Charles's brother Arthur, who had little interest in it and encouraged his son, Francis, to live there. In 1926 Sir Francis inherited Killerton from his father. He was the MP for Richmond, Yorkshire, and his passion was Liberal politics rather than land-owning. He was married to Eleanor, *née* Cropper, a noted left-leaning feminist.

The couple used Killerton as a party house as well as a family home throughout the 1920s, and it became a Liberal stronghold. Over 7,000 Liberal supporters came to a celebration in July 1923, and there were speeches, music, games, fairground rides, food and drink. In 1925, about 20,000 people came to hear Lloyd George launch his land reform campaign from the terrace.

But the Aclands' family life at Killerton was touched by tragedy, when in 1924 their daughter Ellen was killed in a cycling accident on the estate, aged only 10. A disastrous fire the same year badly damaged the east side of the house, and in 1933 Eleanor died. Sir Francis remarried in 1937, but two years later, on the eve of the Second World War, he died.

The Common Wealth Party and the National Trust

On his father's death in 1939, Sir Richard Acland, Liberal MP for Barnstaple, inherited as the 15th Baronet, taking on the role of country landowner with mixed feelings. His wife, Anne Dyke Acland, a qualified architect and polio survivor with a strong personality, shared his misgivings.

Throughout the 1930s, Sir Richard became increasingly left-wing, his egalitarian ideals at odds with his personal wealth and status. His book, *Unser Kampf: Our Struggle*, published in 1940, advocated a blend of Christian socialism with shared ownership of property. It provoked great debate, and as Britain fought against Germany, in 1942 Sir Richard launched a new political movement, the Common Wealth Party, with writer J. B. Priestley, advocating the sublimation of individuals' ambitions to the benefit of the wider community.

Handing over the estate

The new party needed funds to contest by-elections, and the family feared heavy death duties if Sir Richard died. So in 1942 they sold a number of farms and other properties to generate income. Later the same year, Richard and Anne were in conflict; he wanted to sell both Killerton and Holnicote entirely because of his strong political belief in common ownership. But she feared for their tenants, who might end up with exploitative landlords. Eventually they agreed to give the estates to the National Trust.

The acquisition of Holnicote and Killerton in 1944 was represented in the media as a gift, although the National Trust spent £178,000 acquiring the marriage settlement land that had been settled on Anne, paying the commercial rate. The Aclands retained the right to live in the dower house, Sprydon, and also a house on the Holnicote Estate.

Establishment newspapers such as *The Times* questioned Sir Richard's actions as a hereditary landowner, but leftist papers applauded his humanitarian ideals. A man of contradictions, he desired continuity of traditional country life on the estates, but was committed to radical political beliefs. He was generally regarded as a sincere man who had 'given away' his massive inheritance in accord with his personal beliefs. The Common Wealth Party's public support was wiped out by the Labour landslide in the 1945 general election, and Richard lost his seat.

Sir Richard joined the Labour Party, but resigned in 1955 in protest at the H-bomb. He helped to form the Campaign for Nuclear Disarmament in 1957, and turned to teaching. He later became a lecturer for St Luke's College of Education and was delighted when Killerton became a hall of residence for the college in 1963 and he and Anne took on the role of Warden and Wardeness in their old home.

Sir Richard Dyke Acland died in 1990, Anne in 1992. Their eldest son John inherited; he died in 2009. Sir Dominic Dyke Acland, the 17th Baronet, now lives at Sprydon.

Photographs clockwise from top left

Richard with his electioneering car in 1930

Richard with supporters, North Devon election, 1935

Richard and Anne in 1944

Richard canvassing during the North Devon election, 1935

Richard and Anne with supporters, 1935

Richard with farmers on the estate, 1930s

The House and its Collections

When the 7th Baronet engaged the pragmatic and biddable John Johnson as his architect, Killerton House was intended as a temporary residence. But while Sir Thomas mulled over Wyatt's more grandiose plans for a Palladian villa further up the hill, the Acland family got used to the plain and simple stopgap.

Sir Henry Wentworth Acland Baronet (1815 - 1900)
Later Regius Professor of Medicine at Oxford. In 1890 Queen
Victoria created him a Baronet, for his services to Medical Science

Opposite Family photographs on the sidetable in the Staircase Hall

Below right John, Robert and Henry Acland in 1948

Below left Richard, Geoffrey, Cubby and Ellen with Sir Charles Thomas Dyke Acland, 12th Baronet, and Lady Gertrude, Christmas 1917

A change in family fortunes meant that the temporary became permanent and Killerton House grew gradually over the centuries, with additions and alterations to meet the changing circumstances of its inhabitants. Never a slavishly fashionable house, it has followed architectural and stylistic innovations rather than initiated them, but like many a country house it has grown organically and gradually.

Layers of history

Its importance lies not so much in the excellence of its architecture, or the cultural value of its collections, but rather in the layers of history which over the centuries are revealed in the portraits and family stories. Killerton was the vibrant hub of an extensive estate, with many hundreds of people's livelihoods dependent upon the variable fortunes and personal decisions of the Acland family. In later years it was also the nexus of a growing radical political movement which advocated the abolition of personal property. Sir Richard Acland acted on his high-minded principles by giving his estate to the National Trust in 1944 in order to pursue his political agenda, a decision with far-reaching consequences for his family and his tenants.

The Second World War affected Killerton in a material way. Many of the family's possessions were put into store in Exeter for safe-keeping, but unfortunately some were destroyed during the Exeter Blitz of 1942. Consequently, when the National Trust took on the house it was largely unfurnished. Originally it deemed the house to be unimportant and leased the property to a number of organisations, including the Workers' Travel Association (a left-wing body which enabled city families to enjoy rural holidays) and St Luke's College of Education.

Open to visitors

The house was opened to the public in 1978 with the arrival of the Fashion Collection, and was furnished with many loan items, which have been greatly enhanced by furniture and chattels from the Acland family.

Visitors often comment on the domestic, informal atmosphere at Killerton; it still feels like a family house, and as the General Manager says, 'it should smell faintly of dog'. As the building also houses the regional office for the National Trust, parts of the house are inaccessible to the public, but the atmospheric showrooms and the fascinating Fashion Collection grip the imagination.

The Entrance Hall
The Study

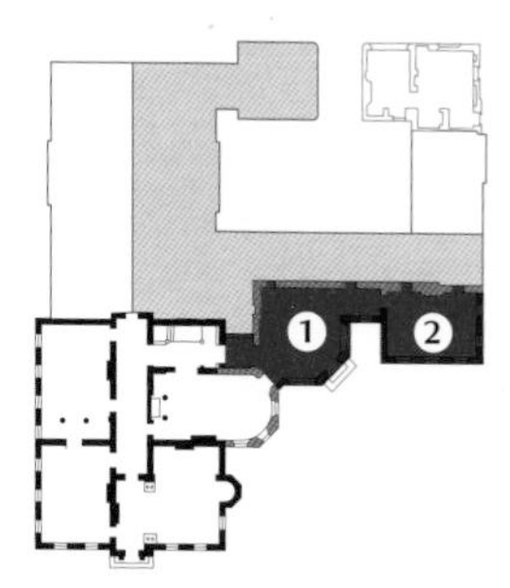

1 The Entrance Hall

In 1924, fire destroyed part of Killerton and, although it was contained, this part of the house was badly damaged. Sir Francis Acland commissioned the architect Randall Wells to design a large entrance hall in keeping with the various activities of a busy country house.

The informality of this setting is attractive – the stone floor and coat-racks were practical measures against new arrivals, possibly

Above The Entrance Hall

Opposite One of the framed Grillion's Club portraits in the Study

Political portraits
The Entrance Hall reflects the Aclands' role at the heart of British political life; in 1813 'Great Sir Thomas' was one of the founding members of Grillion's, a London dining club where politicians of widely differing sensibilities met on alternate Wednesdays to dine together in the agreeable surroundings at Grillion's Hotel in Albemarle Street. He commissioned portraits of the members, and engravings from those portraits hang together in this room.

wearing dirty footwear and wet headgear and mackintoshes. The large oak table was usually covered in newspapers, sports equipment, maps and post. The array of umbrellas and walking sticks, fishing rods, tennis racquets and luggage trunks hints at the busy comings and goings of the family. The chintz curtains and comfortable sofas provided a welcome spot for casual visitors to wait for attention, and it was here that the family would hold informal receptions.

In the 1920s and 1930s, Sir Francis Acland was very active in Liberal politics, opening Killerton for Liberal Party rallies. This passion for politics is reflected in the photographs on display in this room, such as the picture of Lloyd George making a speech to a crowd at Killerton.

2 The Study

Built in 1900, and connected to the Entrance Hall, is a room which recalls the 'bachelor wing' so popular in larger Victorian country houses. Sir Charles Dyke Acland, the 12th Baronet, wanted a billiard room with an area to one side for a 'bookshelf part or study'.

The architect Henry Protheroe created a versatile interior with a fine plasterwork ceiling made from moulds taken from original designs by the Adam Brothers. The doors were of cedarwood from the Holnicote estate, and the walls were painted off-white. It is uncertain to what extent the room was used for billiards; in time the table was moved elsewhere and the room was given over exclusively to business and known as the Study.

A separate Steward's Entrance enabled agents, tenants and workmen to consult Sir Charles in person without entering the main body of the house. When Charles died in 1919, the Study was adopted by the younger members of the family as a sort of den; it was here that they honed their carpentry skills, stored their guns and played darts.

The Music Room

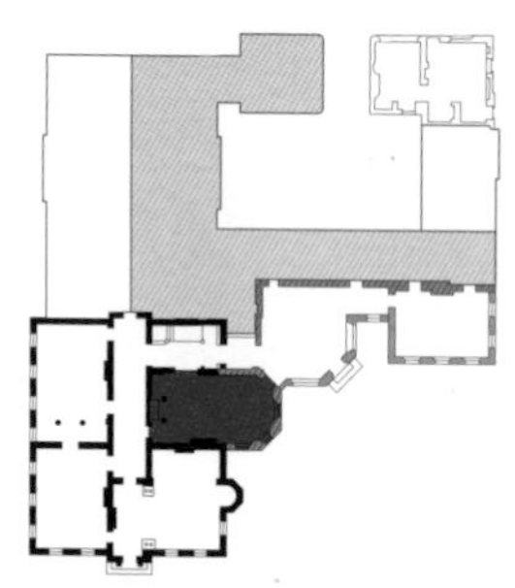

When the house was rebuilt in 1778/9, this was the dining room. The room now takes its name from the chamber organ, built in 1807 for Sir Thomas's wife Lydia.

Lady Lydia's father Henry Hoare, a member of the famous banking family, commissioned the talented and successful organ-maker William Gray to build a chamber organ for his daughter. Lydia was an accomplished singer and harpist, and much of her sheet music survives, complete with scribbled notes. She was taught by S. S. Wesley, the organist at Exeter Cathedral, who wrote six special pieces for her.

Paintings

The portrait of Lady Lydia with their two eldest sons, Tom and Arthur, and their spaniel, Bronte, has pride of place over the fireplace. It was painted by Thomas Lawrence in 1814–15 to mark Lydia's recovery from a serious illness. Other pictures in this room include four charming pastel portraits by Henry Singleton of Lydia's children with dogs. A more formal note is struck by the marble *bas-relief* portrait of Sir Thomas Dyke Acland, the 11th Baronet, over the door to the left of the organ.

Décor and more

The organ is flanked by scagliola columns in imitation of marble, topped with Ionic capitals. At the opposite end of the room, a deep window bay was added, making the room a welcoming and attractive place. The ornate Italian fireplace, dating from the 1840s, is made of four pieces.

The mahogany glazed break-front bookcase opposite the fireplace was made in 1808 by an Exeter cabinetmaker, Mr Carter. Because of its size, it was left at Killerton when much of the Acland's furniture was put into store for

Left This portrait (*c.*1812) by Henry Singleton depicts Lady Lydia playing on the Broadwood piano (opposite)

safekeeping during the Second World War. The bookcase is a rare survivor, as many of the family's most cherished belongings were lost in a bombing raid on Exeter in 1942. The bookcase houses an attractive collection of mostly 18th-century ceramics, including part of a Chelsea dessert service, and French and Oriental pieces.

An informal setting

In the 1920s and 1930s the room was used by the family as a relaxed sitting room for playing games. It was also a favourite spot for gossip, political discussions and afternoon tea. Eleanor Acland was a keen pianist, and when she played the Bechstein, her melodies would gently filter though the adjacent rooms. Visitors are welcome to play this piano.

Above Broadwood grand piano, 1802

Left The Music Room

The Long Corridor
The Drawing Room
The Library

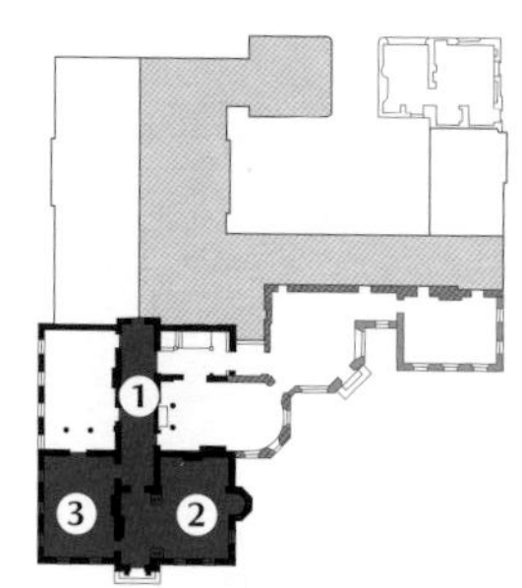

1 The Long Corridor

Simple, broad and handsome, the corridor dates from 1778 and originally led to the main front door of Killerton. Its walls are hung with portraits of Grillion's Club members created by Slater and Richmond. Among their number are such seminal figures as Gladstone, the future Prime Minister; Lord John Russell, who drafted the 1832 Reform Bill; and Lord Ashley, later Lord Shaftesbury, who was responsible for the Factory Acts and the Ragged Schools. In a lit wall-niche is a large silver candlestick from the Club, presented to Sir Thomas in 1846 as a 'Testimonial of Respect'. The elegant George III musical mahogany bracket clock offers a choice of six tunes that are played on the hour every three hours; the selection consists of two 'Jiggs', a song, a minuet, an air and a hornpipe.

2 The Drawing Room

Sir Charles Dyke Acland, the 12th Baronet, commissioned the Drawing Room in 1900. In typical Edwardian fashion, small groups of furniture cluster around the two fireplaces with their ornate inlaid marble surrounds, creating a comfortable and convivial atmosphere. Two chairs flank a Regency combined games and work box with lyre-shaped legs. A typically compact piece of Georgian furniture, it deftly mixes practicality with dainty neoclassical features.

The many paintings in this room include a portrait of Hannah More, the anti-slavery campaigner, who was a friend of the Aclands and of Wilberforce. The painting of Lady Harriet Acland by Robert Pollard (see page 13) recalls her crossing the Hudson River to rescue her husband, Colonel John Dyke Acland, who had been wounded in the American War of Independence.

3 The Library

Originally designed by Johnson as the Little Parlour, this west-facing room was considered too brilliantly lit by Henrietta Acland, who wanted some windows screened. It later served as a drawing room, and was much liked for its peaceful atmosphere and views of the garden.

Sir Charles had the room remodelled as a library in the Edwardian era. In recent years, Killerton has appealed for donations of books relevant to the various interests and pursuits of different generations of the Acland family, from agriculture to Liberal politics. All books on display can be handled and read *in situ*. The only exception is the

Left Bracket clock and framed family photographs in the Long Corridor

Above The Drawing Room

A literary family
A number of family members broke out in print. Sir Thomas, the 11th Baronet wrote the preface to a cookery book, *A Guide to Modern Cookery*, by Mary Harrison. As previously mentioned, Sir Richard wrote *Unser Kampf* and several other political books.

Top right Terracotta roundel by the early 19th-century Danish sculptor Bertel Thorvaldsen

Bottom right Close-up of the false book-backs door in the Library

'false books' to the right of the Dining Room door, where rows of spines bear unlikely titles such as *Crabb on Fishes*, *Wig without Brains* and *Paper Currency Exploded*.

Above two of the doors are terracotta roundels depicting *Night* and *Morning*, low-relief panels by the great Danish sculptor Bertel Thorvaldsen. Lady Lydia Acland played and sang to Thorvaldsen when she and her husband met him in Rome in 1836, and the roundels are mementoes of their Mediterranean travels.

The Dining Room

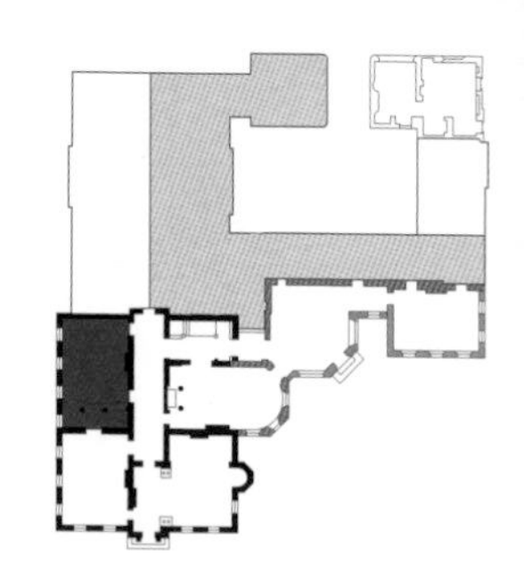

The Dining Room was originally designed by Johnson as the 'Great Parlour' in 1778, and he added his ornamental plasterwork frieze and a pair of carved columns with composite capitals (wooden, but imitating marble) to frame the double doors into the Library and add neoclassical dignity.

Under the 10th Baronet, many a hefty Victorian meal was consumed at Killerton. Dinner was often surprisingly late, embarked upon at 10pm, and it was here that the family and their guests assembled for every meal except afternoon tea, well into the 20th century. Even when it was impossible for the Aclands to retain a butler, two parlourmaids were employed to maintain formal high standards.

The room was redecorated in 2003 and provides a sympathetic setting for significant Acland family portraits. The earliest, of Sir John Acland, the 1st Baronet (*c*.1591–1647), dates from the beginning of the 17th century; Sir John was a Royalist and was granted a baronetcy for his services to Charles I. The portraits commemorate successive generations of male Aclands and the mutually beneficial unions they made with wealthy heiresses, many of whom are also pictured here.

Cold comfort

It is perhaps ironic that, despite their large dowries, the Acland ladies dining formally in this room found it perishingly cold in an era of fashionably bare female shoulders, and hankered to sit on the side of the table nearest the fireplace.

While the late 18th-century mahogany sideboard, probably Irish, is much the same date as the building, the mahogany dining table and chairs are early 19th century. The floor is covered by a very large hand-woven Persian carpet of great geometric complexity.

Left Elegant Ionic columns in the Dining Room

Right The Dining Room with the table set for breakfast

Opposite Portrait of Sir Hugh Acland, 6th Baronet, in the Dining Room

A living death

One of the portraits in the Dining Room is of Sir Hugh Acland, the 6th Baronet (1697–1728), and is a reminder of a legend that arose and was printed in the *Gentleman's Magazine*. Sir Hugh had been taken ill and appeared to have died of a fever. His body was laid out in a coffin. In keeping with the custom, his menservants resolved to 'wait' with the corpse overnight, and they were slipped a bottle of brandy by one of the staff. As the night wore on, they took an occasional nip of alcohol. Probably under the influence, one manservant decided to give his former master one last drink. A tot was poured into the mouth of the corpse; to the attendants' horror, the 'deceased' sat up coughing and spluttering, revived by the brandy. They scattered in terror, raising the grieving household, and Sir Hugh, after being transferred from his coffin to a warm bed, apparently made a full recovery.

The Staircase

As with the Library, it was Sir Charles and Lady Gertrude who wanted the Staircase remodelled to suit their idea of what an Edwardian country house should look and feel like. Gertrude was keen to have a flight of stairs which her well-dressed female guests could descend in style before dinner, preferably attracting the admiration of the gentlemen waiting around the fire below. The resulting oak staircase is rather heavy in effect, but is attractively lit from above from a glass dome in the ceiling with a neoclassical frieze. The impressive alabaster light fitting was designed in the 1920s by Randall Wells, the architect who designed the Entrance Hall following the fire at Killerton in 1924.

Portraits of 18th- and early 19th-century Aclands advance up the stairs. The most prominent is that of *Great Sir Thomas, 10th Bt*, a vast full-length portrait painted in 1818 after his only electoral defeat. Also shown is his adoring and redoubtable wife Lady Lydia.

Right The Staircase was specially designed so that well-attired ladies could show off their dresses as they came down for dinner

The Fashion Collection

On the top landing is the entrance to the fashion exhibition. By a twist of fate, a passionate enthusiast for historic costume, Paulise de Bush, happened upon a cache of wonderful clothes which were on the point of being thrown away. These items form the basis of this important collection.

Origins of the collection

Paulise de Bush (1900–75) was an heiress, the only child of the Baron de Bush, and his opera singer wife, Pauline Joran. When her father died in a bizarre accident in 1903, after falling from a train, Paulise became known as the 'Baby Baroness', as she was the youngest Baroness in Britain. Her love of luxurious clothes and costumes came from her mother, and she collected costumes for her own drama group, the Stockwells Players.

During the Second World War, Paulise became aware that the niece of one of her neighbours who lived in an old house in Aston Tirrold (then in Berkshire, now Oxfordshire) was throwing out vast quantities of period clothes, mostly 18th- and 19th-century dresses, because her uncle was running out of storage space. Paulise bought many items, initially to use as theatrical costumes, but she became fascinated by historic dress in its own right, and began to collect from diverse sources. Her great friend, the theatre designer Atherton Harrison, shared her passion and in 1965 Atherton and her film-maker husband Harvey made a 35-minute film with Paulise, called *Fame and Fashion*, in which Paulise and her models appeared in some of the costumes. In addition, Paulise kept her mother's impressive clothing.

Paulise left a letter with her will which asked Atherton to help find a permanent home for her collection, a place where elements of it could be displayed to the public. Paulise died in March 1975 and Atherton approached the National Trust. Killerton was opened to the public for the first time in 1978, and it was here that Paulise's collection was first catalogued and displayed in a changing programme of themed exhibitions; Atherton continued to act as a consultant until her retirement in 1994.

Opposite Corset designed for a shop display, *c.*1890

Left An elegant portrait of Paulise as a young woman, in which she sports a cropped hairstyle and drop-waisted 'robe de style', early 1920s

Above Paulise de Bush and her grandmother in 1905. Finely pleated silk dresses were worn by wealthy children like Paulise. Her shoes are made of silk satin

Scope and highlights

The costume department at Killerton mounts an annual exhibition of fashion selected from its collection of more than 10,000 items. These represent over two centuries of fashion and textile history.

The exhibits cover all manner of clothing, from court dress to lingerie, stockings to shoes. In addition, there are impressive examples of jewellery, fans, handbags and other accessories. The annual exhibitions are designed to appeal to both the casual visitor and those with more specialist knowledge. Over 50 different items are displayed each year in a sequence of first-floor rooms named after former Acland estates.

The 20th century is particularly well represented, with couture pieces including Fortuny gowns, and outfits by Patou, Chanel and Molyneux. Many of the early 20th-century dresses were worn by Paulise de Bush's mother. The earliest piece in the collection is a man's sleeved waistcoat from about 1690. There are luxury garments as well as fascinating workaday pieces which are rare survivals, including a very well-worn and much-patched set of stays from around 1740–60, made of leather lined with linen, and stiffened by whalebone. One owner expended much energy and skill on repairing and making good her foundation garments; presumably she could not afford to replace them.

The public interest in social and dress history, and the current fascination for vintage fashion, attracts many visitors to Killerton every year. The Costume Curator maintains close connections with fashion and textiles students at a number of colleges, many of whom use the collection as inspiration and a valuable source for practical research. There are even opportunities for visitors of all ages to try on robust replicas of historic hats and garments.

Find out more
Access to the Fashion Collection is limited, but you can see images of many of the items currently in store via the National Trust's Collections Management System at www.nationaltrustcollections.org.uk. There are photographs and details of thousands of items, from dress patterns and ballgowns to underwear and shawls.

Images clockwise from left
Detail of a mantle made from a woollen shawl, 1870–5
Dress and coat designed by Joyce Clissold of Footprints Studio, London, mid-1930s
Striped silk bodice and skirt, *c.*1875
Detail of embroidered velvet and chiffon evening dress, 1924
Back view of braid-trimmed figured silk formal gown, *c.*1780
Sleeve of sack-back gown with matching petticoat, 1765–75
Blue and silver brocade, mid-18th century, altered and said to have been worn by a bride who eloped in the 1780s
Silk pelisse (coat) with 'Tudor' sleeves worn by a bride for her wedding in Chalfont St Giles, 1814

The Laundry

Tucked away at the rear of the ground floor is the Laundry. This is a surprisingly late survival; many country landowners regarded their laundries as essential in the Victorian and Edwardian eras, but it became more difficult to recruit and keep domestic staff as the new century wore on. Many grand houses closed their laundries during the First World War and never re-opened them. At Killerton, however, the laundry employed three full-time female staff and occasional part-timers until 1940.

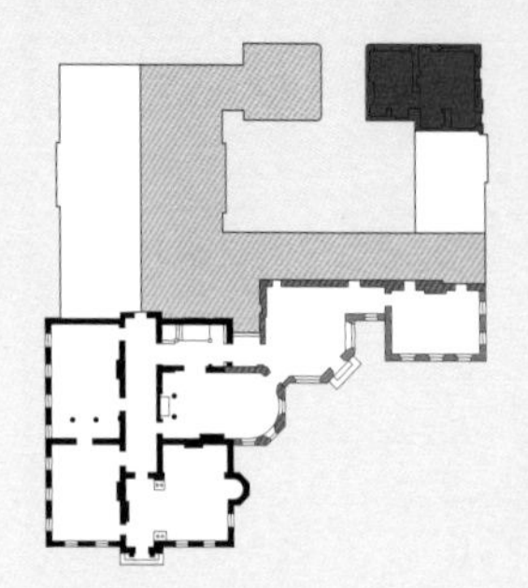

Laundrymaids

The laundrymaids were local girls; one of them, the eldest of six, lived in Broadclyst and joined the Laundry in 1928, at the age of 14. She was paid 18 shillings a week, a big help for her family. The laundrymaids washed all the family's clothes, the servants' uniforms, the household linen and bedding, and there was a huge workload as the Aclands often entertained and had guests staying. Fortunately, the nannies and nurserymaids dealt with the nappies generated by the Acland infants.

The working week

On Mondays the dirty washing was delivered to the Laundry in large wicker baskets. Every item had a tiny identifying label or embroidered code, and was listed in the laundry books accompanying the consignment. Whites and coloured fabrics were separated and assessed for treatment. Throughout the week, particular stains were tackled with a variety of remedies, linens were boiled up with hand-grated soap in two large coppers, and the hand-washing of delicate fabrics, such as silk, chiffon or fine woollens, was undertaken with great care. Wet washing was mangled or handwrung to remove excess water. On wet days clothes and linen were dried on rolling racks in the drying room. Ironing and starching was undertaken at the table under the window, to maximise the available light. In the 1930s, the woman who was responsible for the household linens was paid 4d an hour to iron and starch dozens of damask table napkins.

On Friday afternoons, the fresh laundry was distributed all over the Killerton Estate, according to the code on each item. Ladies' maids, nannies and housekeepers checked off each item in their laundry books, and the hard-working laundrymaids could look forward to their weekend of leisure.

A favoured spot

The Laundry was a popular place for staff, with the housemaids or cook often popping in for a chat. Sir Richard Dyke Acland would occasionally bring each of the laundrymaids a rabbit he had shot, which was appreciated by their hard-pressed families. The Laundry was also the favourite haunt of little Ellen Acland, who was tragically killed in a road traffic accident in 1924. Ellen enjoyed playing with the mangle and would spend hours folding fabric into intricate shapes.

Above Sink and washboards in the Laundry

Opposite The Laundry with its ubiquitous mangles

Below An early 20th-century photograph of Ellen Acland. As a young child, she enjoyed spending time in the Laundry

The Garden and Grounds

Significance and evolution

The main garden at Killerton, as seen today, was created at successive eras in history. Early maps of the site show the old house surrounded by several walled gardens and orchards, a style considered old-fashioned by the Age of Enlightenment. The catalyst was the succession of the 7th Baronet, Sir Thomas Dyke Acland, who wanted an impressive new house set in a carefully romanticised landscape. Between the 1770s and the 1830s, the talented landscape designer and nurseryman, John Veitch, was driven by the desire to create fine views and vistas all over the park and gardens. He used trees and shrubs to dramatic and impressive effect, interspersed with velvety swooping lawns, curving gravel paths, open spaces punctuated by clumps of shrubs, specimen trees, seasonal underplanting such as bluebells, and interesting structures, from a quarry garden to an Orangery.

The important plant collection seen today at Killerton is largely due to John Veitch, who worked here for most of his life, and his descendants. Killerton was the trial ground for many of their introductions. The herbaceous border and decorative terrace beds near the house were largely created in the early 20th century as fashions changed, but overall the garden retains the character of a Regency-era pleasure ground, designed as a place to explore at will and to appreciate aesthetically.

The team today

The garden, parkland and wider estate are looked after by a team of gardeners and countryside rangers who work hard all year round to care for this complex site. They propagate many of their own plants, and maintain the treescape, borders and lawns, in order to care for the gardens in the future according to the high standards of the past.

Opposite This view from the garden towards the parkland reveals the variety of trees and shrubs at Killerton

Below The path leading to the house is edged with immaculate lawns and dotted with specimen trees

John Veitch and his successors

The son of an Edinburgh nurseryman, John Veitch had travelled to London, supposedly on foot, to make his fortune. He was recommended to Sir Thomas Dyke Acland and the two men forged a happy and successful working relationship.

John Veitch arrived at Killerton in 1770 aged just 19, and found it old-fashioned and neglected. Dolbury Hill was bare, stark and unappealing, looming over the H-shaped house. The garden was overrun with weeds and overgrown shrubs, walls were crumbling and the orchard was full of cankered trees. But the estate had a benign microclimate ideal for delicate and semi-exotic plants. In addition its rich, lime-free soil particularly suited camellias, magnolias and rhododendrons, which were just being introduced to Britain.

Designing the park

Sir Thomas sent Veitch to see how the landscape designer 'Capability' Brown was laying out Saltram, the house near Plymouth owned by his friend John Parker. Despite having no previous landscaping experience, Veitch embraced the varied topography of Killerton with enthusiasm. He planted trees to contrast the looming height of the Clump with the gentler slopes of the valley. He favoured naturalised species, such as beech, lime, horse chestnut, sycamore and a variety of oaks, which he cultivated in his nurseries around the estate. The 200-hectare (500-acre) park was punctuated in the idealised fashion of the day by an octagonal folly, and ornamented with a herd of fallow deer.

John Veitch was encouraged and financially supported by Sir Thomas in setting up a commercial nursery at nearby Budlake, and it became a thriving business. Now a respected landscape designer and nurseryman, Veitch was made the agent for the estate in 1779. Sir Thomas died in 1785, the 8th Baronet died as a child and the 9th Baronet kept away from Killerton, so for 23 years Veitch managed the estate. In 1808, 'Great Sir Thomas', the grandson of Veitch's former master, inherited Killerton and was keen to improve it further and the second phase of the transformation began. Veitch helped devise a comprehensive scheme for new gardens, including an underground Ice House, Bear's Hut and the Beech Walk.

Left Over the course of the 19th century, the Veitch family developed one of the largest family-owned nurseries in the country. This is the nursery's Nepenthes house

The Veitch dynasty
After John Veitch's death in 1839 his two sons continued the nursery business, sending plant-hunters to remote places in America and Asia. The Veitch family introduced many new horticultural rarities, often grown or propagated at Killerton for the first time in Britain. Their discoveries and their roles as nurserymen and landscapers profoundly changed the cultivated English park and garden. Killerton is rightly regarded as one of the first arboreta to be established in this country.

Left Wooded glade at Killerton

The treescape

The dramatic setting of Killerton on the slopes of Dolbury Hill invites spectacular planting, and successive landscape designers have enjoyed contrasting the smoothness of the grassy lawns with the imaginative planting of giant trees behind.

Nowadays the stately trees, many of them hundreds of years old, attract visitors to explore the wider park, beyond the area immediately around the house. They appreciate the light and shade and the views, and the majesty of the garden encourages peaceful contemplation.

The **Beech Walk** is a glorious avenue of beech trees running across the side of Dolbury Hill. The **Magnolia area** is spectacular in spring and autumn; one particularly impressive specimen of a *Magnolia campbelli* is so large that it can be seen from three miles away when in flower. Cork oaks grace the upper side of the **Main Grass Path**, and the *Stewartia pseudocamellia* is one of the biggest of its species in Britain. The elegant conifer *Taiwania cryptomerioides* contrasts with the camellias and the incense cedar – tall, dark and distinctively visible from across the valley. It was from the trunk of these trees that cedarwood pencils were traditionally made.

The **Top Path** is lined with massive Wellingtonias (giant redwoods) and is alight with flowering azaleas in spring. Lower down, off the zig-zag path, are two superb sweet chestnuts, planted by Veitch, and a massive California redwood, the tallest tree in the garden, raised from seed in 1843, and planted in 1860. Below is the tree with the widest girth in the garden, another Wellingtonia, planted in 1858. It is named after the Duke of Wellington, 'because it stood above its fellows'.

The first deodar cedar to set seed in this country was planted close to the Chapel, and it was probably the parent of many of the trees in the original Deodar Glen in **Park Wood**. Two tulip trees planted at the same time still flank the Chapel. They were planted by John Veitch as part of the grove of trees to walk through.

Above A deciduous azalea in the garden in May

Left One of the soaring giant redwoods on the estate

Far left The Beech Walk in autumn

Gone with the wind

The prevailing south-west winds can threaten the mature trees in the garden. In 1928 and 1930 (pictured) considerable damage was done to the treescape at Killerton by storms. Shelter belts and wind breaks have been included to diminish the threat, but even so 80 mature trees were lost in the gale of 25 January 1990. It is important to be philosophical about such natural events; great storms can cause much damage, but they also remove weak and elderly plants and trees, allowing new healthy growth in time.

The Terrace
The Bear's Hut
The Rock Garden

The Terrace

Until the end of the 19th century, the garden had been separated from the park by a double row of rhododendrons, and there was a small Italianate garden near the house. In 1905, Sir Charles and Lady Gertrude followed garden designer William Robinson's recommendation to create a new terrace. The beds were filled with many varieties of roses underplanted with herbaceous plants. A massive herbaceous border was also created, over 65 metres long and filled with exuberant plants in the fulsome style made popular by Robinson and Gertrude Jekyll at the time. Robinson also designed a garden of sweet scents, and a lavender walk, both of which were removed by the National Trust. Garden adviser Graham Stuart Thomas later reinstated the border with plants whose colours were selected to be 'cool' at both ends and 'hot' in the centre. The sundial marks the spot where in 1926 Lloyd George launched the Land Reform Bill from the terrace to the 20,000-strong crowd below.

Above The Bear's Hut

Opposite One of a pair of Grecian-style Coade stone urns on the Terrace. They were bought from the famous 'artificial stone manufactory' set up in Lambeth by Mrs Eleanor Coade. Such pieces were in high demand among the landed gentry, who were keen to add a touch of classicism to their idealised landscapes

The Bear's Hut

A rustic structure close to the Rock Garden, the Bear's Hut was built in 1808 by John Veitch on behalf of Sir Thomas Dyke Acland, the 10th Baronet, who was travelling with his new wife Lydia. Veitch was very fond of Lady Lydia. A keen plantswoman, she had taken Veitch with her to visit her relatives at Stourhead, famed for its landscaped park and magnificent specimen trees. Veitch and Sir Thomas planned the hut as a surprise; letters survive from Veitch to his master, listing the progress of the project.

It was built as a delightful novelty – a fanciful hermit's hut, known at the time as the 'Lady Cot', which would act as a summerhouse for the family while they enjoyed the grounds. The hut was constructed of timber from the estate, with a thatched roof. The stained glass in the hermit's window was collected by the Acland family on their travels. Each room is lined with different materials, from varying woods and deer skin, to matting and pine cones, with bark adorning some of the walls. The floor in the inner room is 'cobbled' with deer knuckle-bones, which gardener and writer Jane Loudon described in her influential book *Gardening for Ladies* (1846) as 'decidedly in bad taste'. The hut was renamed because in the 1860s it was used to house a pet black bear called Tom, which had been brought to Killerton by the 12th Baronet's brother, Gilbert, on his return from Canada.

The Rock Garden

Sir Charles and his wife Lady Gertrude had this area remodelled in 1905, instructing their Head Gardener John Coutts to turn it into a contemporary rock garden with alpine plants. A basalt stone column brought back from the Giant's Causeway by the 10th Baronet and his wife Lydia, nearly a century earlier, created a focal point.

In the Edwardian era, the Rock Garden was the great passion of Lady Gertrude, who dedicated four full-time gardeners to its maintenance. It has recently been replanted with Himalayan species, chosen for suitability and their connection with the Aclands: Sir Francis, the 14th Baronet, had sponsored Frank Kingdon-Ward's plant-hunting expedition to the Himalayas in the 1920s.

The Ice House
The Goyle
The Memorial

The Ice House
Cold winters were more common in the early 19th century than nowadays, and fashionable households relied on their ice houses. This one was designed by Veitch in 1808; the structure was built into the back of the quarry, lined with brick, and the exterior was clad in earth and stone to create a natural-looking feature.

During the winter of 1809, 30 men worked for five days to fill it with 40 tons of ice from nearby ponds and the River Culm. The ice was crushed and compacted, and when required, chunks would be broken off with a pickaxe and taken to the kitchen in zinc-lined cases, where it was used to chill bottles and to make the ice-creams and bombes so much in vogue amongst society families.

The Goyle
Near the Bear's Hut is the early 18th-century deer park pale, designed to keep the deer herd in. Originally the pale was formed by a ditch, bank and wall with wooden paling along the top. The wall was faced with stone by unemployed labourers who were laid off when Isambard Kingdom Brunel's Great Western Railway suffered funding problems. As a nearby landowner, Sir Thomas, the 10th Baronet, hired the labourers to give them a respectable living. The structure remains as a wall and planted ditch, forming what is known in Devon as a 'Goyle' – a dark sunken path.

The Memorial

This Memorial in the form of a Celtic cross, listed Grade II, stands on the western boundary of the pleasure grounds. It was erected in 1873 to commemorate the 10th Baronet by 40 of his friends. Their names are inscribed on the base of the cross, and it is evidence of the high regard in which 'Great Sir Thomas' was held by his contemporaries.

The Ladies' Garden

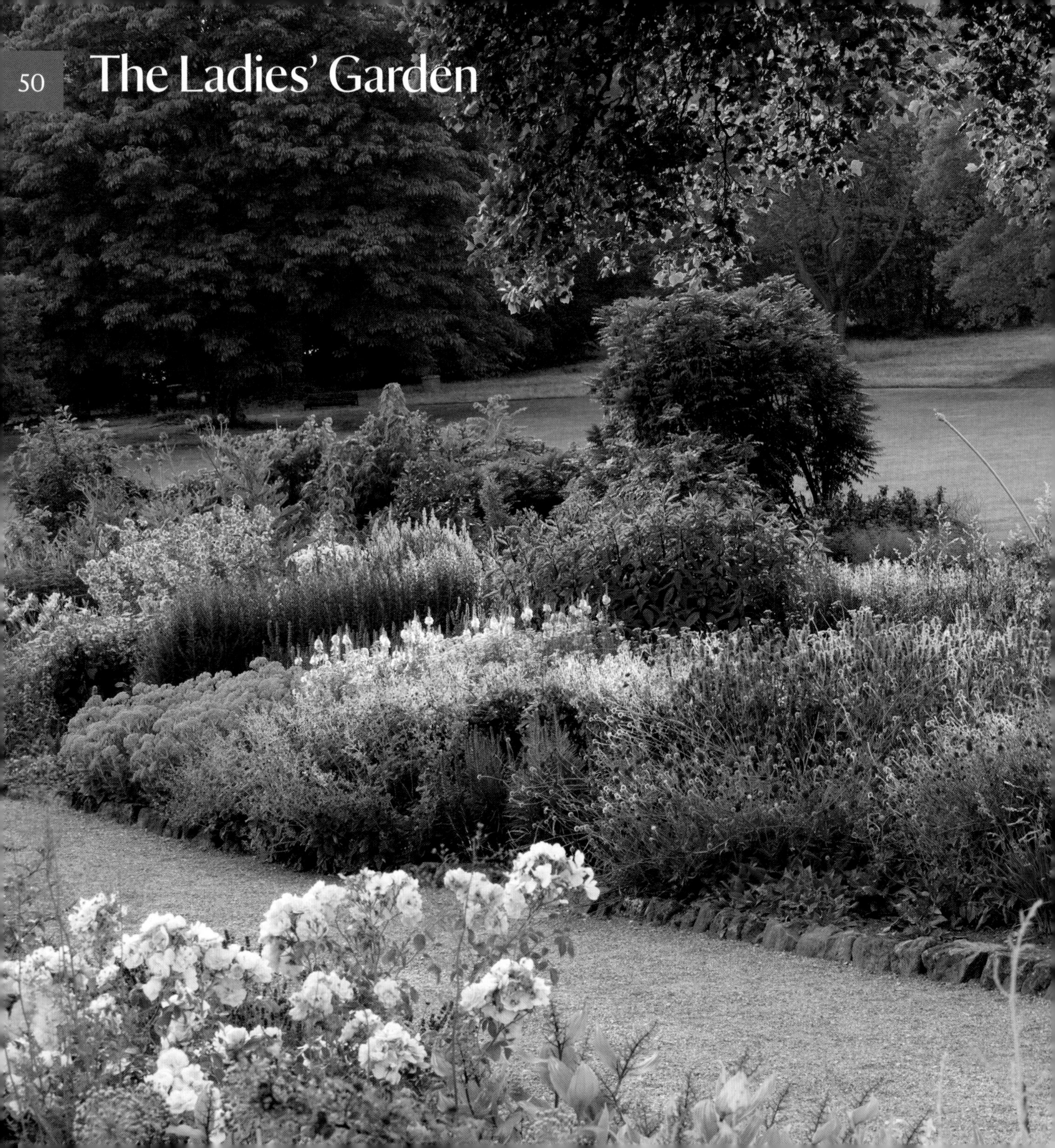

Two Acland ladies had a significant effect on the garden and grounds at Killerton, though their lives there were separated by nearly half a century.

Lady Lydia

Lady Lydia Acland had grown up in Mitcham, a member of the wealthy Hoare family, who owned a beautiful garden. She was a very keen plantswoman, often discussing details with Veitch and exchanging plants with friends and family. In her honour John Veitch created an enclosure near the walled gardens at some distance from the house, known as Lady Lydia's Shrubbery, to be used as a flower garden. It was common practice in this era to enclose flower gardens near to vegetable gardens, and to plant shrubs to disguise their outer walls, so as not to distract from the idealised parkland. This area later became the Chapel grounds.

Lady Gertrude

Lady Gertrude, married to Sir Charles Dyke Acland, who succeeded in 1898, seems to have had a natural affinity with gardening and tended towards an informal, intuitive style rather like that of Gertrude Jekyll. One of her gardeners observed that she would sit in the garden and mull it over before deciding on or abandoning a course of action. He said, 'She could see it as it would be afterwards,' – a rare skill. She had already created an attractive garden during the 20 years she had lived at Holnicote.

Lady Gertrude called in William Robinson, author of *The English Flower Garden* (1883) to advise on Killerton. He recommended a thorough excision of overgrown shrubberies, and the grouping of new trees and plants. Lady Gertrude's Glade of early rhododendrons high on Dolbury Hill was installed, to Robinson's instructions, to provide a spectacular contrast to the magnificent redwoods. In 1905 William Robinson advised removing the double row of rhododendrons which separated the garden from the park. A retaining stone wall was built, and the soil level built up to make a formal terrace, complete with herbaceous borders.

In addition the wilderness at the top of the garden was subdued, and the rock garden was created by the Head Gardener, John Coutts, from the remains of the old quarry. As he left to work at Kew Gardens in 1909, Mr Coutts advised his successor and fellow Scot John Wilson that 'You will find her Ladyship very keen'. Lady Gertrude continued to enjoy her garden even when ill-health confined her to a wheelchair. Many of the azaleas and magnolias now seen at Killerton, as well as the cyclamen and daffodils, were planted at her instigation.

Opposite This herbaceous border is planted in the style of 'wild' gardener William Robinson, who advised on planting at Killerton

Left The rock garden in its heyday

Below The terrace borders were introduced by Lady Gertrude in about 1905

The Chapel

The Aclands were a religious family, and took their duties as role models very seriously. The family had previously used the surviving chapel at Columb John, but that was inconveniently distant in poor weather. So Sir Thomas Dyke Acland (1787–1871) commissioned the renowned architect C. R. Cockerell (1788–1863) to design a grand chapel at the heart of the Killerton Estate.

The architect was better known for his classical style, but he reluctantly agreed to copy the Norman chapel of St Joseph of Arimathea at Glastonbury. The building was completed in 1841 and dedicated to the Holy Evangelists. 'Great Sir Thomas' wanted, and certainly got, an impressive structure.

An unexpected layout

The interior was unusual for an English church, as serried ranks of seating face each other across the aisle, rather than facing the altar. The congregation could all see each other; the Aclands, their guests, their senior servants, their lower servants, their estate workers and the tenants. To Sir Thomas, attending church was a public act of 'witness', and he had a special seat for himself, to underline his central role as benign patriarch, with everyone expected to know their place in the social hierarchy. However, he could also be unorthodox. For instance, he invited the anti-slavery campaigner Samuel Crowther, who afterwards became the first black bishop, to preach at Killerton chapel.

Call to prayer

Sir Charles Dyke Acland, who inherited Killerton in 1898, read the lesson in chapel every Sunday, and shook the hands of his farm tenants after the service. If a tenant did not attend one Sunday, he would send a groom to their house on Monday morning, with a summons to explain their

Below Sketch of the front and side elevations of the Chapel by architect C. R. Cockerell

absence face-to-face with 'Charlie'. These encounters were held in Sir Charles's study, and what might have been a bruising reprimand was always softened by a glass of whisky. Even into the 1960s, estate workers were expected to attend, and the chapel bell rang to call the men to work every morning. Nowadays local choirs sing in the chapel, and give monthly performances between April and September. Weddings are only permitted for members of the parish and a special licence is required.

The Chapel was built in an extension to Lady Lydia's Shrubbery. Near the chapel there are two magnificent tulip trees, planted by Veitch in 1808 – the largest of their type in the country. Cyclamen carpet the ground underneath in January. Veitch also planted the two magnificent hybrid oaks, now over 200 years old.

Left The Chapel's exterior clearly displays its Norman influence

Above The altar and choir stalls

The Stable Block
The Walled Kitchen Garden
The Lodge

Sir Thomas Dyke Acland, the 7th Baronet, was the archetypal 18th-century landowner, and his passion for stag-hunting was second only to his love of horse-racing. He kept racehorses and entered them for the Exeter races from 1772 onwards, competing with his contemporaries including his great friend, John Parker of Saltram. In 1774 Sir Thomas's horse Grecian won the Exeter sweepstakes, bringing him a magnificent trophy, the Exeter Cup, which is on display in the house.

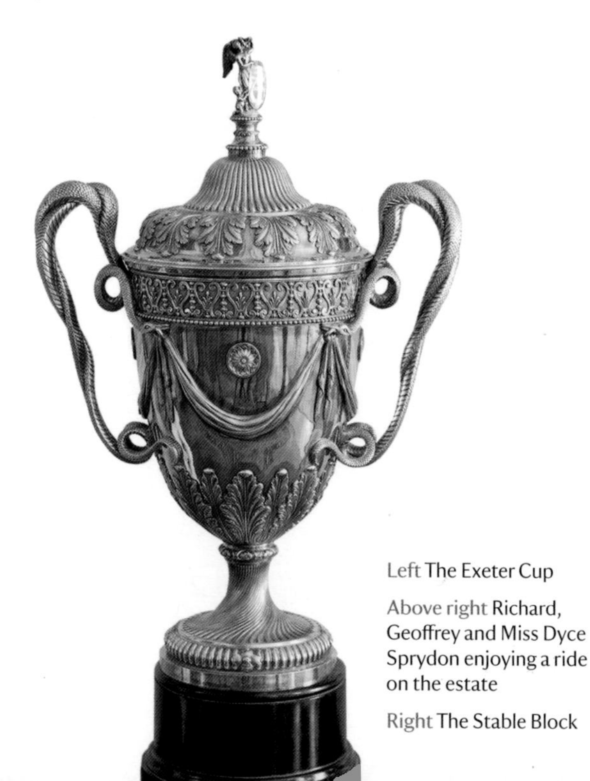

Left The Exeter Cup

Above right Richard, Geoffrey and Miss Dyce Sprydon enjoying a ride on the estate

Right The Stable Block

The Walled Kitchen Garden

The Walled Kitchen Garden was constructed in 1782, close to the Stable Block, approximately 350 metres north-east of the house. Brick walls of approximately three metres high enclose an area now containing ornamental trees, and there was a soft-fruit plantation nearby surrounded by hedges, and a complex of gardeners' outbuildings. The Walled Kitchen Garden now provides car parking for visitors.

The Lodge

The Lodge was designed by C. R. Cockerell, the architect of the Chapel, and was built in 1825 as a single-storeyed stuccoed building to the north of the entrance, flanked by a pair of granite obelisks supporting simple early 19th-century wrought-iron gates. The Lodge provided a decent home for successive semi-retired estate pensioners in return for gate-keeping duties. A young visitor to Killerton in the Edwardian era recalled being met from the train at Exeter by a liveried footman, a waiting carriage and pair, with matching Dalmatian outrunners, and driven to Killerton, where the people of Broadclyst bowed or curtsied at the familiar sight of the carriage. As the carriage approached the gates, the footman blew his whistle and an old lady, known as Granny Baker, hurried to open them. Granny Baker did not pay rent for the Lodge, but her duties encompassed feeding the ducks on the pond.

The Stable Block

The Stable Block at Killerton was commissioned from John Johnson by Sir Thomas Dyke Acland at the same time as the 'temporary' house for the family. However, there was nothing temporary or makeshift about the accommodation provided for the Baronet's beloved horses. Sir Thomas commissioned an imposing structure located some 250 metres from the family home, constructed from dressed Killerton stone salvaged from the house on the hill. The Stable Block was built in a square around a central courtyard, topped with a painted cornice and equipped with a cupola and a new turret clock, which struck the hour and could be heard all over the estate. Nowadays the Stable Block houses the shop, café, plant centre, second-hand bookshop and admissions.

Above View of Holnicote by Francis Towne. Sir Thomas, the 7th Baronet, is depicted returning from a stag hunt with his pack

Right Granny Baker outside the Lodge

Broadclyst Village and the Wider Estate

Budlake Old Post Office

This picturesque, rather compact thatched 19th-century cottage was one of many built on the Killerton Estate by the Acland family to house workers. From 1901 till 1976 the lean-to attached to the cottage housed the sub-post office and village shop, serving local residents.

Nowadays the interior is an evocative mid-20th-century time capsule, with shelves stocked with commemorative tins, boiled sweets in screwtop jars, haberdashery supplies and cleaning materials. The role of the post office as the social hub of any rural community is indicated by the postage stamps, postal orders and dog licences, the postman's uniform, the radio and clock. Visitors can lift the receiver of the Bakelite telephone and dial a number to hear recordings of various local people reminiscing about Budlake Old Post Office.

The Cottage Garden

The Cottage Garden contains traditional flowers such as aquilegias and roses, herbs and a vegetable plot. During the Second World War, like so many others, the garden was largely turned over to vegetables as part of the 'Dig for Victory' campaign. Food rationing continued after the war until 1954, so the garden played a vital role in providing food for its owners. The Skerrett family lived at and ran the post office in the 1950s. Mr Skerrett grew vegetables and fruit, and the chicken coop and pigsty were both used to house livestock. Waste and vegetable matter fed the Skerretts' chickens, who laid eggs for the family to eat. In time, the poultry would also themselves be eaten. Many families in the 1950s also kept a pig, a thrifty way of using household waste, garden refuse and leftovers to provide some extra meat in lean years.

Outdoor privies and washhouses were still much in use in rural communities in the 1950s. At Budlake Old Post Office there is a two-seater privy, and a restored laundry washhouse.

Today the Cottage Garden is looked after and maintained by a dedicated team of volunteers.

The Telephone Box

An icon of British design, the K6 telephone kiosk still standing outside Budlake Old Post Office was designed by the famous architect Sir Giles Gilbert Scott. The K6 was first made available in 1936, and towns and villages with a post office could apply for a phone box to be installed outside their premises. Local authorities paid £4 for a five-year subscription, and the local telephone kiosk was a lifeline in isolated communities where private domestic phone lines were an unaffordable luxury.

Opposite Budlake Old Post Office features the distinctive yellow colouring of many of the houses on the estate

BUDLAKE
POST OFFICE

TELEPHONE

TELEPHONE

Coins Not
Accepted Here

PULL

Broadclyst Marker's Clyston Mill

Broadclyst

The village of Broadclyst is part of the extensive Killerton Estate; a number of domestic buildings are rendered with Killerton's distinctive yellow limewash, using indigenous clay. A local paper described Broadclyst as 'the Sunshine Village' when the estate resumed using the yellow limewash. Farm buildings and outbuildings in Broadclyst tend to be rendered with limewashes tinted with the stronger red colour derived from the iron-rich local soil.

The Aclands owned property in the village for about 400 years before it was taken on by the National Trust. The family built the vicarage for one of their younger sons and worshipped in the church. Many Aclands are buried there, including Sir John Acland, who bought the Killerton Estate in the early 17th century; his tomb graces the interior of Broadclyst Church. Ellen, the only daughter of Sir Francis Dyke Acland, is buried in the churchyard and inside the church a stained glass window is dedicated to her memory.

Community life

The Killerton Estate owns the school, the hairdressers, the post office, a restaurant and the Red Lion pub. There is a community orchard in the centre of the village, and allotments are available for local tenants. A recent venture is the Broadclyst community farm. When a lease came up for renewal in 2010, as the leaseholder wanted to leave, the farmhouse was rented out separately and the land and outbuildings were taken on by a group of local people, shareholders who invest time and money cooperatively, and jointly pay rent to farm the land.

Marker's

Marker's is a remarkable survival, a late medieval house of the type once found throughout the area, and probably dates from the late 15th century. The cottage owes its name to a former owner, Sarah Marker, who lived here between 1790 and 1814. Originally there was an open fire in the central hall, and

Above The Hall at Marker's

Opposite left to right
Brian Kirby, miller at Clyston Mill, pours cleaned wheat into a wooden hopper

Ursula Kirby, miller at Clyston Mill, tests the consistency of newly milled flour

Chef at Killerton, with a tray of loaves made on site

Left Sampler in Marker's

its smoke gradually blackened the nearby timbers. One window has never been glazed; before industrialisation window glass was an expensive novelty for many country folk. The internal space was subdivided into a hall and parlour by a plank-and-muntin screen, for which the cottage is well known. Rare vernacular paintings on the oak screen, executed around 1530–50, depict a cherub and a picture of St Andrew.

Clyston Mill

Clyston Mill is a picturesque and historic water-powered mill, situated on the River Clyst and surrounded by farmland and orchards. Organic grain is ground at the Mill to make flour, which is used in the home-made bread and cakes at Killerton's restaurant.

Left Clyston Mill

The forests and the wider estate

The broader estate has maintained many of its original features such as hedgerows, and the landscape is varied, containing woods, wood pasture and farmland trees, fen, flood plains, streams and wetland areas. Public access to these areas is well provided, with many miles of footpaths, cycle tracks and also bridleways through Ashclyst Forest, Danes Wood, Paradise and White Downs.

Ashclyst Forest

Ashclyst Forest is one of the largest areas of woodland cared for by the National Trust, and one of the largest forests in East Devon. It is home to a wide variety of trees with glades and heath, criss-crossed by several trails, all clearly marked, and consequently very popular with walkers. The range of ground-growing flora is diverse, sheltered by historic, semi-natural woodland, and the forest is internationally important for its lichens. The garden and woodland area along with the rivers, ponds and buildings provide a unique habitat for over seven species of bats which are carefully monitored.

The forested hill is topped by Wellingtonias, bought in by the Acland family in batches of 12 during the Victorian era. This was where John Veitch had his nursery, and veteran trees are still nurtured. Woodland management is vital to the maintenance of the forest as it is sustainable and provides a great environment for wildlife.

Ashclyst Forest is a key site for nature conservation, providing a home for the pearl-bordered fritillary butterfly, one of the much-threatened UK Biodiversity Action Plan Priority Species. Ancient trees harbour several species of bat, including the very rare barbastelle, as well as hole-nesting birds, and regionally important wood decay invertebrates.

Above Ashclyst Forest

Images clockwise from top left
Greater spotted woodpecker

Pearl-bordered fritillary

Buzzard

Nuthatch

Caddihoe

Caddihoe with its grazed wood pasture shows how much of the countryside looked before the enclosures of the 18th century. It now provides a home to Exmoor and Dartmoor ponies, as well as Angus and Devon cattle. Parts of Caddihoe are now run as commercial forestry, with larches and oaks. Softwoods are grown to provide biomass fuel for local businesses, a carbon-neutral form of fuel, as trees take in carbon dioxide, and give out oxygen. Carbon dioxide is released when the wood is burnt, but reabsorbed by replacement trees. Charcoal burning provides some revenue for the estate; charcoal for barbecues is sold in the shop. Low-grade wood is thinned out, stacked and seasoned, then burnt in a kiln to make high-quality charcoal.

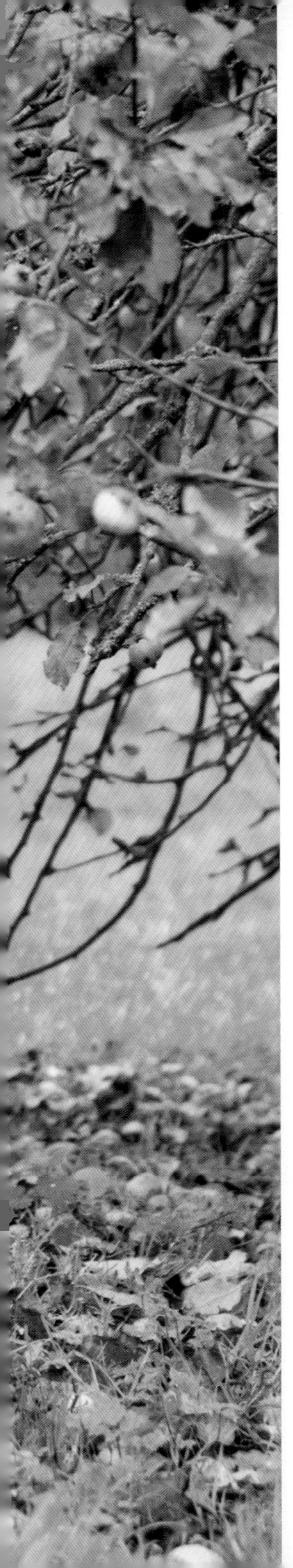

Food and produce

As a working agricultural estate, Killerton needs to develop its potential resources, exploiting all aspects of its varied produce. Timber is an important resource for the estate. The extensive mixed forest was planted by the Aclands on the less fertile land as a long-term investment, and the National Trust now harvests the timber in a sustainable manner.

Timber

The estate sells around 1,000 tonnes of surplus timber each year. The best quality timber is sold as building materials. A proportion of the by-products are used as fuels in biomass, and 300 tonnes a year is sold as logs for domestic woodburners. The estate also prepares on site its own high-quality charcoal, which is sold in National Trust shops.

Agriculture

Agriculture provides approximately one-third of the estate's income. Farm tenants are encouraged to supply the restaurant at Killerton; Ashclyst Farm provides the restaurant with organic milk, and Burrow Farm produces organic beef, while the community farm in Broadclyst supplies many of the vegetables. Wild roe deer are culled on the estate to protect growing trees and the venison is used in the restaurant.

Left A volunteer collects apples in one of Killerton's orchards

Right Cider from the estate

Orchards

Traditional food and beverages are actively marketed by the estate. This part of the world has always been famous for its apple orchards, as the soil is fertile, the climate is mild, and the valleys sheltered. The orchards at Killerton cover more than 20 hectares (50 acres) and are home to over 100 different varieties of apple, including local ones such as 'Killerton Sweet' and 'Killerton Sharp'. The estate team currently produce 6,500 litres of cider each year and also make apple juice, both of which are sold at Killerton. Estate staff use an ancient hand-cranked cider press which pre-dates Whitworth, who standardised the size of nuts and screws in 1841, so a local blacksmith has to custom-make replacement mechanical parts if the original components break.

In October every year, Killerton holds apple weekends, with volunteers helping to pick up windfall apples from the orchards. These are washed and put through the apple mill, and the resulting juice is placed in huge tanks and fermented till late May. The restaurant staff also make their own apple chutney to use up surplus apples. The orchards encourage bees to pollinate the trees, and the honey is harvested and also sold through the shop, creating a virtuous circle.

Sustainability and small-scale production is encouraged and local growers are able to deliver their fresh produce a short distance to the Killerton Estate, thereby avoiding transportation costs and 'food miles'.

The Future of Killerton

Killerton is a fascinating and complex estate, some 2,500 hectares (6,200 acres) of land with a unique and special character.

The Aclands had a well-deserved reputation as benevolent landlords. The sense of community continues today in the relationships with the 20 tenanted farms, with the estate workers living in cottages in Broadclyst and through the development of strong links with the local village.

The 250 estate buildings, many of them vulnerable and made of traditional materials, need investment to keep them maintained. The annual budget for day-to-day maintenance of the houses, cottages and farm buildings currently exceeds £450,000 per year.

The garden and estate are one of the South West's most attractive countryside destinations, with a blend of historic parkland, farmland, ancient woodlands, traditional orchards and rolling Devon countryside. The estate has a network of more than 60 miles of permissive footpaths and cycle tracks, and Killerton is working alongside Sport England on the best way to promote walking, running and cycling for all. The National Trust is keen to promote Killerton for family recreation, with orienteering courses, leisure cycle tracks and a weekly family running event. The Killerton Estate will be even more important to the nearby city of Exeter and its inhabitants in the future, as the Cranbrook development will bring new housing to the edge of this rural estate with its ancient woodland and glorious landscape.

Below A family enjoys a leisurely cycle ride on the estate